The ABCs of Costa Rica

Dedicated to my Aunt Ree
for always supporting me in all I do.

My husband Jose and our family, Ana Gabriela, Miguel, Gabriel, Sol, Pietro, Fer, María José, Ricardo, Angie, Iván, Sara, Julián, José María, Mariano, Tomás, Lucy, Ana María, Breeah, Tessa, and so many more I wish I could list.

My host family Lili, Abraham, Verónica, Chichi, and Adri.

You all are the roots to my tree of love for Costa Rica.

The ABCs of Costa Rica: A Travel Guide For Kids

Copyright © 2024 Casey Edmonds

All rights reserved. No part of this publication may be reproduced, distributed, or transmitted in any form or by any means, including photocopying, recording, or other electronic or mechanical methods, without prior permission of the publisher.

Illustrations by Karina Taylor
Book Design by Zoe Mellors

ISBN: 979-8-9895879-5-7 (Paperback)

ISBN: 979-8-9895879-4-0 (Hardcover)

First edition 2024

The ABCs of Costa Rica

A Travel Guide For Kids • A Travel Guide For Kids

Casey Edmonds Karina Taylor

So you're going to Costa Rica
There's so much to do and see
Want to hear some cool things?
Follow me

From A all the way to Z.

Aa

Hop on the avión, let's take off!

First stop: Alajuela

Visit the aguas termales
They're near Volcán Arenal,

Oh, and don't miss the beautiful
Wa-ter-fall!

avión	airplane
aguas termales	hot springs
Volcán Arenal	Arenal Volcano

B b

Lots of people travel by bus [boos]

You can too!

If you're going to Limón you might see a banano tree, it's true!

bus
bus

banano
banana

bloqueador
sun block

The sun is strong, and I don't want you to be sore, So, bring lots of bloqueador! [bloh-kay-ah-door]

In Costa Rica they use **colones**,
That's the currency.

Drinking **café** is part of their culture,
it grows there like a tree.

You can try a **casado**,
visit **Cartago**,
Or try canopy!

One more thing I can't leave out,
it's a fruit you've never heard about…
Cas is the name, and once you try it
you'll never be the same!

colones	currency
café	coffee
casado	typical lunch
cas	fruit

Dd

Costa Rica has become a popular **destino** so **diay**!

What are you waiting for, **let's go!**

Destinos populares

- Manuel Antonio
- Monteverde
- Río Celeste
- Guanacaste

destino destination

diay well

Ee

Do you know what it means to be **eco-friendly**? If you don't then visit this country.

Check out what Costa Rica is doing to save the planet:

They use renewable energy.

They educate their people about sustainability.

They recycle their waste.

They protect their forests.

F f

Yummy *frutas* in Costa Rica you will find,
Try them all if you don't mind.

Costa Rica is glad you came,
Enjoy some *fresco* while you watch the *fútbol* game!

Costa Rica's *fútbol* teams:

Deportivo Saprissa

La Liga Alajuelense

Club Sport Herediano

frutas
fruits

fresco
fresh fruit juice

fútbol
soccer

Gg

What is that you say?

Guanacaste
[Wan-uh-kos-tay]

That's a province that will make you want to stay.

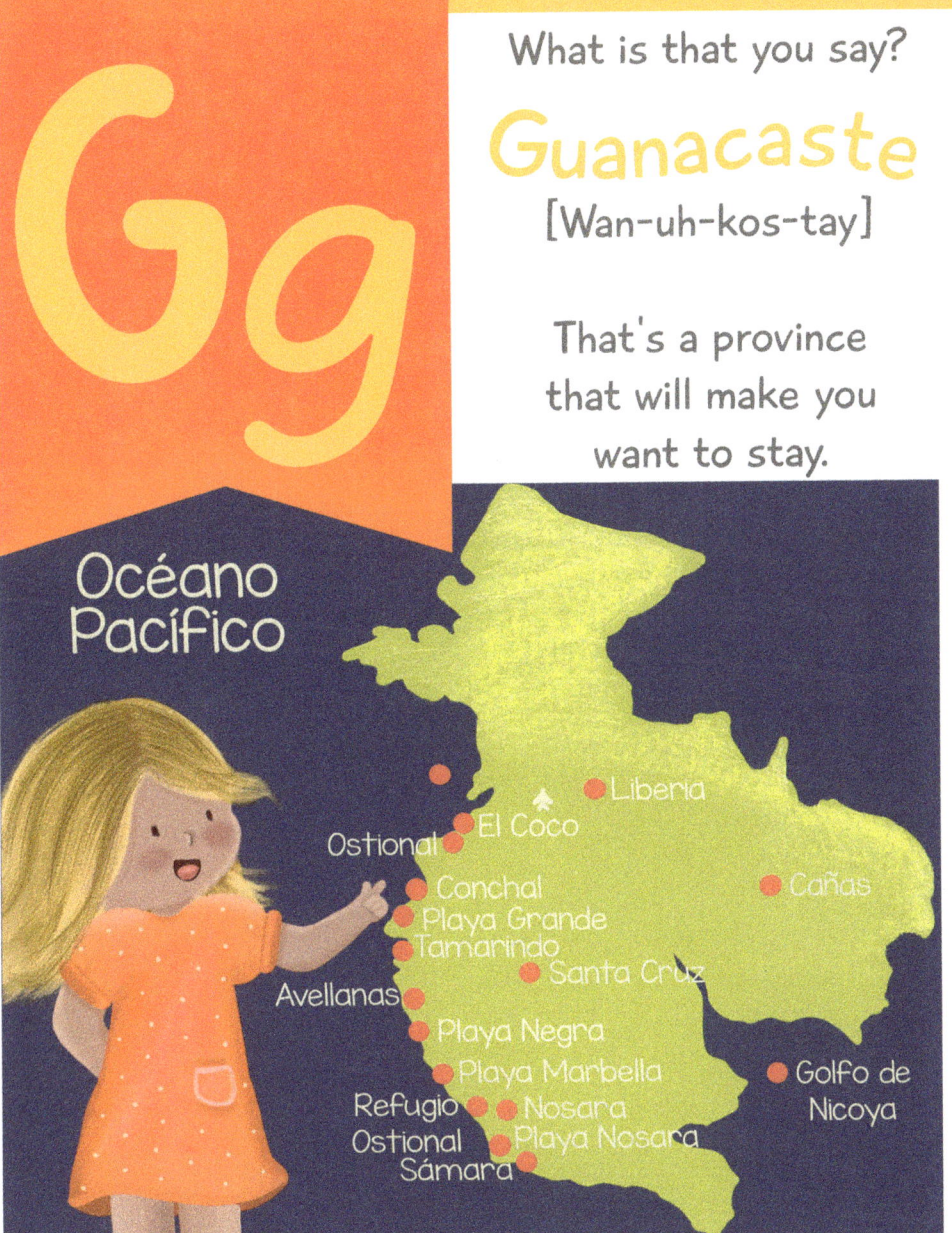

Beautiful beaches for you to play
Don't forget
the national dish,
gallo pinto,
to start your day.

gallo pinto
typical Costa Rican breakfast

Hh

It's very **húmedo**,
didn't you know?
You'll still like it though.

Find a nice **hamaca**
to lay
And there you can
pass the day.

I recommend **Heredia** for part of your stay.
Things to do in Heredia:

Café Britt   Volcán Barva

húmedo
humid

hamaca
hammock

Places to stay:
Casa del Café

Ii

A volcano just for you
Its name is **Irazú**
Hike around and take
in the view

J j

Many visitors travel to **Jacó** [Hah- koh]
It isn't a place I love to go

¡Jale a otro lado! [hah-lay]
Visit **page 5** for recommendations.

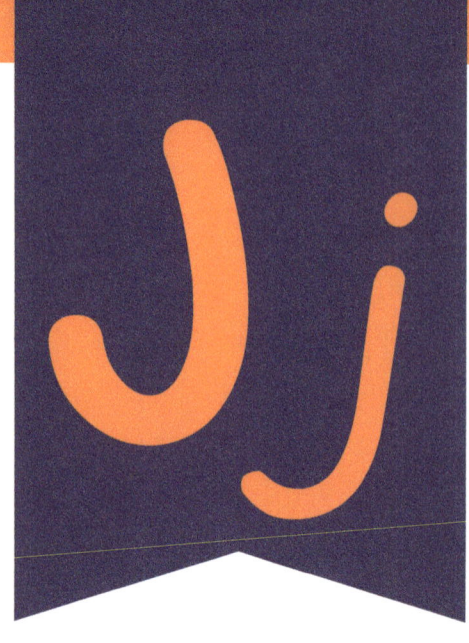

¡Jale a otro lado!
Let's go somewhere else!

K k

How far will you go? Your distance in Costa Rica is measured by the kilómetro.

Did you know only 3 countries aren't using the metric system?

kilómetro
kilometer

Ll

Remember back on page 3
When I mentioned the banano tree?
You'll see them in Limón
A province many animals call home

banano
banana

Don't miss the:
Jaguar Rescue Center

M m

Mariposas, mariposas fly
Maybe you can see them
in **Monteverde** if you're
passing by

Atop the trees,
there's lots to see
Was it cool?
Send a picture to me.
Send photos to be
featured on the
author's site:
edmondscb4845@gmail.com

Me regala is what you say
When ordering stuff from day to day
If you hear **mae** [my] it means dude
It wouldn't be polite to say it when
ordering food

mariposas
butterflies

Me regala
Can I have?

mae
dude

N n

Naranjo, a village nestled in a mountain Can help you find your zen

Once full of orange groves Now there aren't too many of those

Check out:
Chayote Lodge

Have you ever seen an

o soooo pere zo sooo??

They move so
sloooooow
You can find them
in a few places
And take a picture of
their cute faces

Sloth breeds in Costa Rica:

Hoffman's
two-toed sloth

Brown-throated sloth

oso perezoso
sloth

Pp

What type of traveler are you?

For adventure seeking...

White water raft on Río Pacuare [Pa-Kwa-Ray] Class III and IV rapids, what do you say?

Río Pacuare
Pacuare River

playa
beach

piñas
pineapples

pulpería
small family-owned store

Pura vida
hi, hello, good morning, bye, see you later, thank you, cool, or the direct translation of pure life!

For the relaxing type...

Go to the playa in Puntarenas
Munch on papayas and piñas
You can find them at the pulpería

Don't forget Costa Rica's motto when you're leaving: **Pura vida.**

If you go to Quepos [Kay-pose] you might just stay there,
Rainforest, beach, and eat in a plane if you dare

If you do
This is the saying you'll want to view

¡Qué chiva!   It means how cool!

Pro tip:
Keep your food secure, the monkeys are near

Check out El Avión Restaurant

Río Celeste,
a real natural beauty
Where two pieces of water meet
If you go here you may leave with muddy feet.

Río Celeste
Celeste River

Ss

San José is the capital
It's not very tropical
The **selva** is another place
That goes at a slower pace

I can't leave out the **soda**
I'm not talking Coca Cola
A **soda** is a small place to eat
Usually run by families you'd be happy to meet

selva
jungle

soda
mom and pop restaurant

T t

Costa Ricans are also called **ticos**
They say **toque, tuanis,** and **todo bien**
Tico time is why they're late
For almost every date

Don't miss the turtles of **Tortuguero**
But this will depend on the time of year you go

ticos
Costa Ricans

toque
moment

tuanis
cool

todo bien
all is well

Green turtles in Tortuguero
(July - October)

Leatherback turtles in Guanacaste
(October-February)

U u

Usted [oo-sted] is the formal way to say you In Costa Rica they use it more than tú Are you an older kid, lady, or lad?

Consider studying abroad at Costa Rica's universidad.

tú
informal way to say you

usted
formal way to say you

universidad
university

V v

You can find a volcán
In many parts of
their land
Check out some of
the popular ones
Known to man

volcán
volcano

¡Wakala! Ewww!

Some ticos might say
What did you do
to make them feel
this way?

You blew your nose at the table
So please, go to the bathroom,
if you're able

wakala
disgusting

ticos
Costa Ricans

Xx

X marks the spot.
Look at the map and
mark an X on the sites
in Costa Rica
You want to visit

Yodo means coffee, did you know?
It's been a great souvenir since long ago

Get it for friends or family
So they can sip their joe happily

Author's recommendation for coffee: 1820

yodo
coffee

Zz

Wherever your family goes
There may be zancudos
[san-koo-dohs]

You won't only see those
Zaguates [sag-wa-tays] are there too,
I must disclose

zancudos
mosquitos

zaguates
stray dogs

Sponsor a Costa Rican zaguate:

https://donate.territoriodezaguates.com/

Aa Bb Cc
Dd Ee Ff
Gg Hh Ii Jj
Kk Ll Mm
Nn Oo Pp
Qq Rr Ss Tt
Uu Vv Ww
Xx Yy Zz

About the Author

Casey Edmonds, mom, teacher, and longtime lover of all things Costa Rica first discovered the amazing country when she went to study abroad in 2008. It didn't take long for her to fall in love with the pura vida lifestyle.

Since then, she's been back countless times—in fact, she could even be there right now!

About the Illustrator

Karina Taylor is a children's book author and illustrator from Costa Rica, based in the United States. She has illustrated puzzles, books for different publishers, independent authors, as well as her own books. With a whimsical style, she is so passionate about bringing characters to life.

You can visit her website www.illustratekari.com

Other Books By
Casey Edmonds

No More Milk on the Savannah:
A Story about Weaning

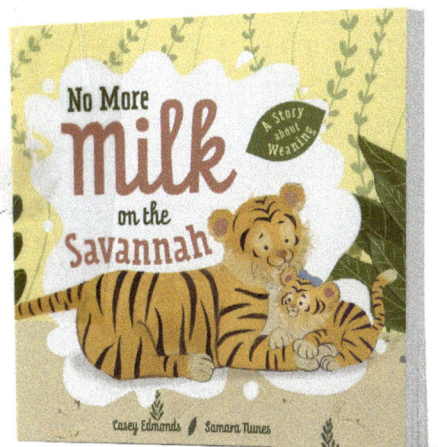

Tess is a nursing cub who loves Mama and her milk. The only problem is that Mama's supply is running low. Feeling frustrated and upset, Tess must find other ways to bond with Mama.

Follow Tess on her journey as she overcomes her challenge of weaning off Mama's milk.

Available now on Amazon!

No más leche en la sabana:
Un cuento para el destete

Tess es una cachorrita que ama amamantarse de su mamá, a la que quiere mucho. El único problema es que la leche de mamá se está agotando. Frustrada y triste, Tess tiene que encontrar otras maneras de establecer vínculos afectivos con su mamá.

Sigue a Tess en este viaje emocional mientras vence el reto de dejar de tomar la leche de mamá.

Costa Rica

A	T	N	D	S	E	L	V	A	F	O	A	O	R
M	A	E	A	U	R	E	M	D	R	N	C	C	Ó
N	E	Z	A	G	U	A	T	E	E	I	A	A	A
R	A	T	A	L	I	M	Ó	N	S	T	O	O	Z
R	C	A	R	T	A	G	O	N	C	S	B	T	D
O	A	C	O	N	N	S	U	G	O	E	A	A	Z
D	I	A	D	Ó	A	U	S	T	E	D	N	S	A
A	H	M	O	C	Y	R	T	P	S	T	A	O	N
E	E	A	Y	I	O	A	A	I	L	U	N	P	C
U	R	H	D	E	A	S	N	N	C	A	O	I	U
Q	E	A	D	O	O	A	R	L	J	O	Y	R	D
O	D	B	I	T	U	S	I	E	M	O	S	A	O
L	I	A	A	T	N	S	O	D	A	Ó	A	M	F
B	A	P	Y	N	A	S	A	T	U	R	F	E	S

HAMACA   NARANJO   PLAYA
ZANCUDO   FRUTAS   BLOQUEADOR
TUANIS   ZAGUATE   USTED
CARTAGO   HEREDIA   MARIPOSA
YODO   LIMÓN   DIAY
CAS   BANANO   TICOS
MAE   SELVA   DESTINO
FRESCO   SODA

Play this puzzle online at: https://thewordsearch.com/puzzle/8399751/

My Costa Rican Adventure

_____ are going to _____, Costa Rica.
      (Who)   (Place in Costa Rica)

While we're there we're going to _____.
                                            (activity)

That will make us super _____ so then we'll probably
                            (adjective)

_____. We will have to try _____.
   (verb)   (food/drink)

It looks sooo _____.
                             (adjective)

It's very possible that we'll also end up _____.
                                               (verb+ing)

I can't wait!

After trip....

We did it! It was _____!
                                 (adjective)

If you get a chance to have a Costa Rican adventure you should

try _____, _____, and _____.
    (thing/activity)   (thing/activity)   (thing/activity)

www.ingramcontent.com/pod-product-compliance
Lightning Source LLC
Chambersburg PA
CBHW040231110526
44582CB00001B/18